O9-BHL-750

momentum for life leader guide

michael slaughter

momentum for life
leader guide

Biblical Principles for Sustaining
Physical Health, Personal Integrity, and Strategic Focus

ABINGDON PRESS
NASHVILLE

MOMENTUM FOR LIFE:
BIBLICAL PRINCIPLES FOR SUSTAINING PHYSICAL HEALTH,
PERSONAL INTEGRITY, AND STRATEGIC FOCUS—LEADER GUIDE

Copyright © 2008 Michael Slaughter

All rights reserved.

No part of this work may be reproduced or transmitted in any form or by any means, electronic or mechanical, including photocopying and recording, or by any information storage or retrieval system, except as may be expressly permitted by the 1976 Copyright Act, the 1998 Digital Millennium Copyright Act, or in writing from the publisher. Requests for permission should be addressed to Abingdon Press, P.O. Box 801, 201 Eighth Avenue South, Nashville, TN 37202-0801, or e-mailed to permissions@abingdonpress.com.

This book is printed on acid-free paper.

All Scripture quotations unless noted otherwise are taken from the Holy Bible, TODAY'S NEW INTERNATIONAL VERSION®. Copyright© 2001, 2005 International Bible Society. All rights reserved throughout the world. Used by permission of International Bible Society.

Scripture quotations noted (NRSV) are from the New Revised Standard Version of the Bible, copyright 1989, Division of Christian Education of the National Council of the Churches of Christ in the United States of America. Used by permission. All rights reserved.

Scripture quotations noted (KJV) are from the King James or Authorized Version of the Bible.

ISBN 978-0-687-65263-1

08 09 10 11 12—5 4 3 2 1
MANUFACTURED IN THE UNITED STATES OF AMERICA

contents

A Word to Leaders

Momentum for Life is a six-week study for groups desiring to build momentum that will propel them forward into God's promised future for their lives. Written by Michael Slaughter, the study focuses on biblical principles for sustaining physical health, personal integrity, and strategic focus in life. A participant's Workbook provides the basic information and tools participants will need to successfully complete the study; and a separate, personal Participant DVD Journal provides bonus supplemental materials that will greatly enhance the experience.

The Workbook has been designed to help participants get as much out of the study as they possibly can. Each week's lesson includes personal reflection questions within the reading material, as well as "Momentum Builders" at the end of the lesson. Because participants will be invited to share some of these responses with the group, they should complete each week's material prior to the corresponding group session. (Note: Be sure to distribute copies of the Workbook in advance and instruct participants to read and complete Week 1 before the first group session.) Remind participants that they alone are the ones who will determine whether or not this is just another group study or a transformational experience that will have a dramatic, positive impact on their lives.

The Participant DVD Journal is another tool to involve your group members in the content and the disciplines of *Momentum for Life*. Especially good for those who love to be online or who travel with their computers, it includes extra content such as one-on-one video from Mike Slaughter and friends, guided prayer loops to help in daily devotion time, journaling pages to record weekly progress, and more. A free preview copy for you is included in the back of this book. For use on DVD-enabled computers, this interactive devotional journal is a great way to draw participants to a deeper level as they learn the practices outlined in this study. As you prepare for each week's session, there will be a helpful hint for you to point out to those who chose to use this valuable resource.

Whether or not your group meets in a church, a home, or another setting, all you need to facilitate the weekly sessions is this Leader Guide, the Group Session DVD, a TV and DVD player, and a chart or board and appropriate writing instrument for group activities. Because no two groups are alike, this guide has been designed to give you flexibility in tailoring the sessions for your group. You may use the following suggested format, *or adapt it as you wish to meet the schedule and needs of your particular group.* (Note: The times indicated within parentheses are merely estimates. You may move at a faster or slower pace, making adjustments as necessary to fit your schedule.)

Suggested Format	**(45-60 minutes)**
Icebreaker	(5 minutes)
Video	(6-10 minutes)
Group Discussion	(20-25 minutes)
Application Exercise	(10-15 minutes)
Accountability Assignment	(1-2 minutes)
Closing Prayer	(1-2 minutes)

Here are a few helpful hints for preparing and leading the weekly group sessions:

Read and complete the material for the week in the Workbook and, if possible, watch the DVD segment. In the "Preparing for the Session" section at the beginning of each weekly session, you will find brief summary information about the DVD segment for that particular session.

Select the specific discussion questions you plan to cover. Highlight these or put a checkmark beside them. (For 20-25 minutes of discussion time, it is suggested that you select 5-7 questions.) A "Session Planning Page" is provided at the end of each weekly session. Use this page to make notes through the week as you pray and prepare for each session.

Secure a TV and DVD player in advance; oversee room setup.

Begin and end on time.

Be enthusiastic. Remember, you set the tone for the class.

Communicate the importance of accountability groups to this study. If at all possible, determine the accountability groups prior to the first group session. Depending upon the total number of participants, assign 3-5 people to each accountability group. Then create a list of names, e-mail addresses, and phone numbers for each group. Distribute copies of the lists during the "Accountability Assignment" time of the group session, or have participants break into accountability groups and exchange contact information at that time. Encourage the groups to pray for one another and exchange words of encouragement each week and throughout the entire study.

Create a climate of participation, encouraging individuals to contribute during the "Icebreaker," "Group Discussion," and "Application Exercise."

If no one answers or responds at first, don't be afraid of a little silence. Count to seven silently; then say something such as, "Would anyone like to go first?" If no one responds, venture an answer yourself. Then ask for comments and other responses.

Model openness as you share with the group. Group members will follow your example. If you share at a surface level, everyone else will follow suit.

Draw out participants without asking them to share what they are unwilling to share. Make eye contact with someone and say something such as, "How about someone else?"

Encourage multiple answers or responses before moving on.

Ask "Why?" or "Why do you believe that?" to help continue a discussion and give it greater depth.

Affirm others' responses with comments such as, "Great" or "Thanks" or "Good insight"—especially if this is the first time someone has spoken during the group session.

Give everyone a chance to talk, but keep the conversation moving. Moderate to prevent a few individuals from doing all of the talking.

Monitor your own contributions. If you are doing most of the talking, back off so that you do not train the group to not respond.

Remember that you do not have to have all the answers. Your job is to keep the discussion going and encourage participation.

Honor the time schedule. If a session is running longer than expected, get consensus from the group before continuing beyond the agreed upon ending time.

Consider involving group members in various aspects of the group session, such as asking for volunteers to run the DVD, read the closing prayer or say their own, and so forth.

Before each group session, pray for God's presence, guidance, and power; and throughout the study, pray for your group members by name and for what God may do in their lives. More than anything else, prayer will encourage and empower you as you and your group seek together to build momentum for life.

Let's get started!

Week 1
Momentum: Mass in Motion

Week 1
Momentum: Mass in Motion

Preparing for the Session

Watch the DVD segments that you will view with participants this week, Introduction (3:15) and Momentum Busters (18:45).

Introduction: In this short introductory segment, author Mike Slaughter introduces the need for discipline and "self-leadership." He says, "You must be able to lead yourself before you can lead other people." Mike is the senior pastor of a large church and uses church ministry examples as he offers tangible ways to describe leadership, momentum, and burnout.

He explores the idea that time for new beginnings comes again and again in our lives. "I believe that there is one new birth but there are many conversions through our lifetimes and where I want to challenge you today is in some of those areas in your life where you need conversion."

"God isn't going to trust you with a new thing or give you more responsibility until we practice what we already know."

Momentum Busters: This video segment comes from a sermon series Mike preached at Ginghamsburg UMC on finding momentum in your personal and professional life. From this introductory sermon in the series, he highlights the momentum busters of defaulting, being overwhelmed, and disorganization.

This video segment runs longer than other weeks, so you may not have time to view all of it. Below are listed several key sections; some time markers are also provided to help you find these.

Mike says, "Holiness is a commitment to whole-life living where every area of our life becomes an honorable, excellent offering to God.

The areas in our life where we are stuck are less than an honorable, excellent offering to God" (0:51).

Mike discusses the effects of procrastination, "Failure in your life comes in direct proportion to what you put off to do tomorrow what you know you need to do today" (1:35).

"How long will you lie there, you sluggard? When will you get up from your sleep? A little sleep, a little slumber, a little folding of the hands to rest—and poverty will come on you like a bandit and scarcity like an armed man" (Proverbs 6:9-11).

Mike talks about how we can all experience changed behavior to live a better, more energized life. He says, "Here is why procrastination is so bad. It doesn't just affect today, it attaches itself to your psyche, your subconscious and it will reproduce itself in your life years later...you will literally because of procrastination thirty years ago, dream of panic, failure, and defeat" (3:49).

He then discusses the Three Characteristics of Procrastination:

1. *Defaulting*: work on non-urgent, comfort activities. You make a commitment to do the right, urgent task in your life but you default to a less urgent task or comfort activity (5:48).
2. *Overwhelmed*: there is so much to do that you cannot get started. "You have to make a commitment to do the first hard thing" (8:42).
3. *Disorganization*: cluttered spaces anywhere in your life create cluttered thinking which creates cluttered spirits which create cluttered lifestyles. God is a god of order (14:00).

"Nothing worthwhile is easy. You have to make the commitment to do the first, hard thing." Mike shares his own difficulties when, at forty-nine, he began trying to get in shape. Realizing that all leadership begins with self-leadership, he knew he had to begin to exercise and change his lifestyle. In any area where you are stuck, you need someone to lead. He didn't know where to start and realized at last that he needed a coach.

"You can't lead beyond where you are. You need someone who is ahead of you to lead."

Disorganization in your personal, spiritual, financial life will grow. God is a God of order. "When you are in disorganization, you need a life map, and a life map is a critical plan with a definite starting point in hard places" (15:25).

Participant DVD Journal: You may also want to familiarize yourself with the Participant DVD Journal that participants are encouraged to use in their personal time. You may wish to share the following tip with participants choosing to use this resource:

TIP ONE: Week One on the DVD contains supplemental materials to the Introduction we discussed this week. Delve deeper by completing a Status Check of D-R-I-V-E in your daily walk. There is also an opportunity to identify potential Momentum Busters that can slow down your progress. Each week Mike Slaughter has a special, motivational message for you and there is a beautiful Prayer Loop to encourage you to spend time in prayer.

Icebreaker (5 minutes)

Draw two columns on a board or chart. Label one column "Momentum Builders" and the other "Momentum Breakers." Then ask the group to name highly publicized individuals, groups, and/or companies who have maintained positive life-momentum when faced with challenges, obstacles, or problems (Momentum Builders), as well as those who have not (Momentum Breakers). (Refer to page 8 in the Workbook for some examples.) List the names in the appropriate columns as they are mentioned. Which list is longer?

Video (6-10 minutes)

(Running Times 3:15, 18:45)

Group Discussion *(20-25 minutes)*

Note: More questions are provided than you will have time to cover in the group session. Select from those provided to suit the needs and interests of your particular group.

1. Share your definitions of *self-leadership* (Workbook, p. 9). Why is self-leadership so important to all progress, positive influence, and leadership in general?

2. Why do you think so many people give up on their God-given dreams, settling for a job instead of a life calling?

3. What does it mean to say that faith—the Christian life—is a journey of ascent? Read Psalm 122. How is our journey of faith similar to the journey of the Israelite worshipers to the holy Temple in Jerusalem?

4. Why does God allow "resistance" in our lives? What can help us to deal with our tendency to rationalize that we are the exception—that we can achieve the desired goal without all the effort?

5. Share your answers to the question, *Why do you think that rationalizing in one area leads to rationalizing in every area of life?* (Workbook, p. 16).

6. Read Romans 12:1. What does it mean to offer every area of our lives as a holy and pleasing offering to God? How can the equation "Faith + discipline = momentum for life" help us to do this?

7. Read Proverbs 31:10-31. According to these verses, how does this amazing woman reflect momentum in every area of D-R-I-V-E?

8. Read Proverbs 6:9. In what ways does procrastination lead to poverty? Share examples from your own life as you are willing.

9. What are the two primary ways that we procrastinate, and how can we overcome them?

10. What can help us to take that first hard step?

11. Why is vision so important to the journey of faith? Read the following Scripture verses: Proverbs 29:11; Psalm 122:2; Philippians

3:13-14. What can we learn from these verses about vision/visu-
alization?

12. Discuss the following statement: *Grace is active: Our sweat meets
Jesus' blood, and that's where the miracle takes place.*

Application Exercise (10-15 minutes)

Read the following aloud: *We all practice rationalization and procrastination at one time or another. We need to deal with our big "buts"—the big
procrastination statements we use on ourselves. Time—or the lack of it—is
often our biggest excuse. "But I don't have time to get close to God," or "But
I don't have time to exercise because I'm too busy." The truth is, if we're too
busy for D-R-I-V-E, then we're defaulting to lesser tasks.*

Ask: *What's your biggest "but" right now?*

Participants may refer to their responses on page 18 in the
Workbook. Invite them to share their responses with the group. Take
notes so that you may mention the various reservations in the closing
prayer.

Accountability Assignment (1-2 minutes)

Prior to the group session (if possible), organize participants into
accountability groups of 3-5 people (depending upon the total number of
participants), and create a list of names, e-mail addresses, and phone
numbers for each group. Distribute copies of the lists at this point of the
session, or break participants into accountability groups and have them
exchange this information. Encourage the groups to pray for one another
during the week and, as they are able, to share words of encouragement
before the next group session.

Closing Prayer (1-2 minutes)

Dear God, thank you for assembling this group of individuals who
desire your best for their lives. We commit today—both to you and to one
another—to give our all to this study so that we may begin to build

momentum for life—momentum that will propel us into your promised future for our lives. Lord, we lift up to you our specific reservations, rationalizations, and excuses; and we ask for your help in overcoming them . . . (*name specific prayer requests now*). From this day forward, may we stop defaulting to lesser tasks and take time for the things in life that are truly important. Amen.

Key Components of Session: Start Time

_____ _____

_____ _____

_____ _____

_____ _____

_____ _____

_____ _____

_____ _____

Three points I want to make:

1. _____

_____

_____

2. _____

_____

_____

3. _____

_____

_____

Prayer Requests:

_____

_____

_____

_____

_____

_____

Week 2
Devotion to God

Week 2
Devotion to God

Preparing for the Session

Watch the DVD segment that you will view with participants this week, Devotion to God (5:02).

In this segment, author Mike Slaughter describes the first discipline in his five-step momentum plan, D-R-I-V-E—daily devotion to God.

Hey says, "The first discipline of my day is to meet with God in Bible study, meditation, journaling, and prayer."

"It only takes me about 24 hours to lose a healthy fear of God. If I'm not using the written Word to listen to the living word, I'm dangerous. I am susceptible to spiritual viruses."

Mike describes, quoting from Carl Jung and Richard Foster, how the speed prevalent in our culture creates a constant sense of hurry that can inhibit us from deeper thinking and prayer. Devotion renews our ability to think more deeply, clarifies direction, and helps us meet the resistance we face in our daily life.

"God speaks to people because they are listening. God is more interested in you knowing the right direction than you are in hearing."

Mike also explains his daily devotional method, S.O.N., using verses from a reading from 1 Samuel 17 as an example:

Scripture – reading the scriptural text
Observation – making observations about the text
Name – naming the applicable principles

After the Scripture work, he then writes out his prayer for the day. (Note: The book Mike describes using with the whole congregation is the

23

Transformation Journal: A One Year Journey Through the Bible [Abingdon, 2007].)

Participant DVD Journal: You may also want to familiarize yourself with the Participant DVD Journal that participants are encouraged to use in their personal time. You may wish to share the following tip with participants choosing to use this resource:

TIP TWO: This week, begin to incorporate the S.O.N. Method into your daily routine. You will find a helpful format to use on the Participant DVD Journal. You can also spend additional time exploring Donation vs. Sacrifice—go ahead and test yourself! Plus, view another message from Mike Slaughter and spend time in prayer.

Icebreaker (5 minutes)

Ask participants to name their passions—what they are most enthusiastic about; what they devote their time, energy, and resources to. If one or more group members already know someone in the group, have them try to name that person's passions before the individual reveals them.

Video (6-10 minutes)

(Running Time 5:02)

Group Discussion (20-25 minutes)

Note: More questions are provided than you will have time to cover in the group session. Select from those provided to suit the needs and interests of your particular group.

1. Read 1 Samuel 13:14 and Acts 13:22. What do these verses tell us about David? How does David's life illustrate the power of our passions—for good and for evil? What can we learn from his example?

2. Read Matthew 4:1-11. Why did Satan direct his attack toward Jesus' human passions rather than his cognitive beliefs?

3. Why do you think our passions, more than our beliefs, determine our life actions and directions? How has this been true in your own life?

4. Why is it our *passion* for God, rather than our *belief* in God, that must grow if we are to have the momentum we need to thrive in the face of resistance? What are some ways we can grow or increase our passion for God?

5. Do you agree that God is always speaking but we're not always present to the relationship? Why or why not?

6. Has it ever seemed to you that God was hiding? Looking back, can you now see that God was with you in ways you simply were not aware of at the time? Share as you are willing.

7. What does it mean to be fully present to God's presence? Share your answers to the question, *What helps you to focus on God's presence?* (Workbook, p. 28).

8. What is the great temptation for any child of God making the journey of ascent to the House of God? What are some of the "gods of immediacy" that tempt us to stop short of true transformation and seek mere relief?

9. What do Psalm 121:2 and Jeremiah 3:23 remind us? How can a daily devotional practice help us to resist the temptations of the "sirens" that call to us?

10. Read Genesis 32:22-30. What can we learn from Jacob's example? What does it mean for us to "wrestle with God," and why is this important?

11. Read Luke 9:23-24. What does Jesus call us to do? What does this involve? What is the promised result? How is this kind of lifestyle different from the lifestyle promised by the world?

12. Read Mark 1:35. Why do you think devotion was the first discipline of Jesus' day? How can we profit from following his example? What are some of the obstacles that threaten to keep us from

beginning the day with devotion, and how might we overcome them?

13. Why is it important to have a specific method or practice that guides your daily devotion? How could the S.O.N. Bible study method help to connect you to God's presence and purpose each day?

Application Exercise (10-15 minutes)

Break into accountability groups and share popcorn responses to the questions: *What is your "danger zone"? What passion has the potential to "take on a life of its own," tempting you toward idolatry?* (Workbook, p. 30). Then discuss ways you can begin to increase your passion for God.

Accountability Assignment (1-2 minutes)

Invite accountability groups to pray for one another in regard to their "danger zones" throughout the week and to encourage one another to try one or more of the ideas they discussed for increasing their passion for God.

Closing Prayer (1-2 minutes)

Loving God, we acknowledge that it is our passion, not our belief, that drives our worship and directs our lives. We don't need to increase our belief or our faith; we need to increase our passion for *you*, O God! Help us to steer clear of the "sirens" that call to us, tempting us to seek immediate relief. Empower us day by day to choose the life of the sacrificial servant, not the life of self-gratification. May we be disciplined in our devotion to you, seeking to be fully present to your presence each and every day. Amen.

Key Components of Session: Start Time

_____   _____

_____   _____

_____   _____

_____   _____

_____   _____

_____   _____

_____   _____

Three points I want to make:

1. _____

_____

_____

2. _____

_____

_____

3. _____

_____

_____

Prayer Requests:

_____

_____

_____

_____

_____

_____

Week 3
Readiness for
Lifelong Learning

Week 3
Readiness for Lifelong Learning

Preparing for the Session

Watch the DVD segment that you will view with participants this week, Readiness for Lifelong Learning (5:03).

In this video segment, author Mike Slaughter asks, "How do I stay relevant for God's purpose to be relevant to the culture to which I'm ministering? How am I staying relevant in the most critical mission for God in a culture that is changing this quickly?"

Mike describes reading in cross-disciplines in order to learn and grow in new ways, using Moses' knowledge of Egyptian culture and law as an example of being ready to be used by God in unique ways.

"We need to daily stretch our minds, as well as our hearts and spirit, so we can be relevant in the culture we live in. What we study becomes the ideas that are translated into action."

Mike describes learning about media and the impact new media was having on the way people learned. Asking where people are receiving information today led Mike and his leadership team to change the way worship was designed and led in his church. What Mike read and studied became what he was leading in his congregation. Mike also makes a brief reference to how reading regularly about the Sudan crisis led to a major ministry project. (To learn more about what they are doing in Darfur, visit http://ginghamsburg.org/sudan.)

Mike discusses how we can pursue wisdom through:

Personal experience
Others' experience
Wisdom of the ages

Proverbs 1:20 says, "Wisdom calls aloud in the streets."

Participant DVD Journal: You may also want to familiarize yourself with the Participant DVD Journal that participants are encouraged to use in their personal time. You may wish to share the following tip with participants choosing to use this resource:

TIP THREE: This week take time to learn about more lifelong learners and be inspired to try some new things—no matter your age! Also explore lots of online resources that can point you to ways to become a lifelong learner. Plus, view another message from Mike Slaughter and spend time in prayer.

Icebreaker (5 minutes)

Read the following aloud:

On the journey of ascent, the best is always yet to come. God calls us to be lifelong learners so that we never stop contributing to God's dream for the world. Consider these lifelong learners:

- *At age fifty-nine, Michelangelo learned a new method of painting upside down and painted* The Creation of Adam *on the ceiling of the Sistine Chapel.*
- *At age sixty-six, Colonel Harland Sanders started the Kentucky Fried Chicken chain.*
- *At age sixty-nine, Ronald Reagan was elected to his first term as president, the oldest person to be elected president until he topped his own record and was re-elected at seventy-three.*
- *Nelson Mandela became the first black president of South Africa at age seventy-five after being a political prisoner for twenty-seven years.*
- *John Glenn made his second trip into outer space at age seventy-seven.*
- *Grandma Moses took up painting in her seventies and created her most famous painting,* The Old Checkered House, *at age eighty-two.*

Is there someone you know who inspires others that the best is yet to come by his or her own example?

Invite each participant to name a lifelong learner he or she knows personally (perhaps a family member, neighbor, or friend) and *briefly* tell how this individual has been inspirational.

Video (6-10 minutes)

(Running Time 5:03)

Group Discussion (20-25 minutes)

Note: More questions are provided than you will have time to cover in the group session. Select from those provided to suit the needs and interests of your particular group.

1. If God intends our work to be fruitful and fulfilling, why do you think many people view work as duty or drudgery—a necessity that is not enjoyable? Why do you think so many people remain in jobs they do not enjoy?

2. What does the author suggest is the key to work that is both fulfilling and fruitful? Share your responses to the question, *How can the regular discipline of lifelong learning help your life to be more fruitful?* (Workbook, p. 42).

3. What does it mean to "exercise" or "stretch" your mind? What are some ways you can do this? How does stretching your mind help you to make an honorable, excellent offering to God?

4. Read Romans 12:1-2. What does it mean to renew your mind? How is renewing your mind like stretching your mind? What does verse 2 say is the result of renewing your mind?

5. Read Genesis 2:15. How does the concept that we were created to be co-creators with God impact your understanding of work?

6. Why must we keep our minds flexible if we are to be used by God? How does Matthew 9:17 relate to this idea?

7. Review the paradigm shifts discussed on pages 44–45 in the Workbook. Name a specific paradigm shift that has been challenging to you personally. In what ways have you been required to stretch your mind in order to embrace this new idea, technology, or practice?

8. What does having a commitment to excellence mean for us as Christians? Who sets the standard for us? How does the saying "the best is yet to come" reflect a biblical perspective?

9. Share your responses to the question, *What is one way you can pursue the excellence of God in your work/service?* (Workbook, p. 48).

10. How is work an act of worship? In what ways do you render service to God through your daily work?

11. Read Psalm 127. According to this psalm, what is vain labor? What does John 6:27 say we are to work for?

12. What is the difference between a job and a calling? As you are willing, share your responses to the questions about your passion/dream on pages 49–50 in the Workbook.

13. When we are actively participating in the redemptive work of Jesus, what should be the result or outcome of our labors? How can we help to ensure that our work is a poured-out sacrament?

14. In what ways did Jesus demonstrate innovation as he went about doing the work of God? How would you describe an *innovator*?

15. Discuss the three practices of lifelong learning and how each one can help us to keep moving forward on the journey of ascent. Which one is most challenging for you personally, and why?

Application Exercise (10-15 minutes)

Break into accountability groups and discuss the following: *What has been feeding and inspiring you lately? What have you read, observed, or done recently that has helped you to grow or move forward? How has it benefited you?* In conclusion, have each person name one thing he or she will read, observe, or do in the coming week to stretch his or her mind.

Accountability Assignment *(1-2 minutes)*

Suggest that as participants stretch their minds in the coming week, they also share something of interest with the other members of their accountability group. It might be something they find inspiring, informative, or instructional. E-mail is an excellent and efficient way to do this.

Closing Prayer *(1-2 minutes)*

Gracious God, it is not your will that we toil in vain, anxious labor. You desire our work to be fruitful and fulfilling. Yet we must be intentional about sustaining a childlike attitude, always continuing to learn and grow, if we want to enter into the fruitfulness of kingdom living. Teach us how to stretch our minds and practice the discipline of lifelong learning, so that all of our work will be an excellent and honorable offering—an act of worship that glorifies you and blesses the lives of others. May we commit ourselves each and every day to the practice of learning and always keep moving forward, remembering that the best is yet to come. Amen.

Key Components of Session: Start Time

_____ _____
_____ _____
_____ _____
_____ _____
_____ _____
_____ _____
_____ _____

Three points I want to make:

1. _____
_____
_____

2. _____
_____
_____

3. _____
_____
_____

Prayer Requests:

_____
_____
_____
_____
_____
_____

Week 4
Investing in Key
Relationships

Week 4
Investing in Key Relationships

Preparing for the Session

Watch the DVD segment that you will view with participants this week, Investing in Key Relationships (9:10).

In this segment, author Mike Slaughter explores the way many people postpone and set aside the most important relationships in their lives in order to accomplish deadlines, tasks, and other priorities.

"We know how to come into church with happy faces like everything is okay and we are dying on the inside." Mike, a pastor himself, says that clergy particularly seem to use their ministry to postpone their relationships.

Isaiah 5:8 says, "Ah, you who join house to house, who add field to field, until there is room for no one but you, and you are left to live alone in the midst of the land!" (NRSV).

Mike shares a crisis that he and his wife, Carolyn, met in their own marriage. He says, "We came to a place where Carolyn said to me, 'I'm not playing this game anymore. This is a lie. People in our church began seeing this. June 1, 1992, we are taking six months and we are either going to get divorced or we are going to commit all the way.' "

Then he says, "Jesus is Lord of both of our lives—and if Jesus is in charge of her life and Jesus is in charge of my life and we can't make this work, it is nothing but sin. We by faith acted as if we loved each other . . . From June 1, 1992, we placed our relationship and our family ahead of the church. Not ahead of Jesus but ahead of the church."

Mike outlines the commitments for key relationships:

- Reserve some 'margins' in your life—time for people closest to your heart.

- Make time for the people most strategic to your ministry for God. Mike talks about the people important to his ministry as a clergy person—who are the people in our lives that are part of our own ministry?

Participant DVD Journal: You may also want to familiarize yourself with the Participant DVD Journal that participants are encouraged to use in their personal time. You may wish to share the following tip with participants choosing to use this resource:

TIP FOUR: This week, examine the Relationship Rituals in your own life and think about how you can develop some with your own family and friends. There are also helpful, online resources to explore that will give you ideas on how to develop these rituals. Plus, view another message from Mike Slaughter and spend time in prayer.

Icebreaker (5 minutes)

Invite each participant to name or *briefly* describe a meaningful relationship ritual in his or her existing family or family of origin, including what makes it significant to him or her.

Video (6-10 minutes)

(Running Time 9:10)

Group Discussion (20-25 minutes)

Note: More questions are provided than you will have time to cover in the group session. Select from those provided to suit the needs and interests of your particular group.

1. What serves as a reminder of life's true meaning? Why do you think we tend to lose our focus on what really matters when things are going smoothly in our lives? What can help us to keep our focus on the most important things in life?

2. What are relationship rituals? Share your responses to the question, *What are the relationship rituals in your family/extended family in which you find meaning?* (Workbook, p. 60).

3. What happens when we do not make relationships a priority in our daily lives? What happens when we do?

4. Share your responses to these questions: *What was the last crisis that caused you to realize you are not in control? Did you take any positive steps toward the people in your life at that time; and if so, what were they?* (Workbook, pp. 60–61).

5. Discuss the following statement: *Life is not about the stuff we own or our personal accomplishments; life is about people.* As you are willing, share some experiences that have helped you to realize the truth of this statement.

6. Read Psalm 128. According to this psalm, what happens when the object of our devotion is right?

7. Is it strange to think of your work and your relationships as your truest demonstrations of worship? Why or why not?

8. What are "margins," and why do we need them in our lives? What are some of the things we allow to fill our margins that keep us from devoting time to relationships? Discuss some practical ways we can create and maintain margins for the key relationships in our lives.

9. Read Matthew 6:34 and James 4:14. What are the implications of these verses?

10. What is the difference between ideals and values? What are the truest indicators of our values?

11. Why is it important to make our families a higher priority than our work, our hobbies and interests, and other relationships? Practically speaking, how can we do this in our fast-paced, high-pressure world?

12. Share your responses to the question, *How are you choosing to invest in your key relationships—the people in your heart?* (Workbook, p. 68).

13. Regardless of our professions or work, what is the one priority we all should share? What does it mean to "build people," and how does this contribute to God's mission in the world?

Application Exercise *(10-15 minutes)*

Divide into accountability groups and discuss ways to create and maintain margins for relationships in your daily lives. Share what has worked for you—and *not* worked for you—in the past, as well as new ideas you might try. Commit to create margins in your life this week for at least one key relationship.

Accountability Assignment *(1-2 minutes)*

Challenge participants to be intentional and specific in scheduling margins for at least one key relationship this week. Instruct them to share a brief "progress report" with the other members in their accountability group before the next group session. Encourage them to pray for one another and, as they are able, to offer words of encouragement to one another during the week.

Closing Prayer *(1-2 minutes)*

Creator God, you made us for relationship—relationship with you and with one another. We thank you for the gift of family and friends. It is in the context of these relationships that we experience life and find meaning. Yet so often we fail to make relationships a priority in our day-to-day lives. Help us to create and maintain margins in our lives—open spaces and time for investing in the lives of others. Remind us that when we do this, we honor you and participate in accomplishing your work in the lives of others. Bless our efforts to create margins and invest in relationships this week, Lord. Amen.

Key Components of Session: Start Time

_____ _____

_____ _____

_____ _____

_____ _____

_____ _____

_____ _____

_____ _____

Three points I want to make:

1. _____

_____

_____

2. _____

_____

_____

3. _____

_____

_____

Prayer Requests:

_____

_____

_____

_____

_____

_____

Week 5
Visioning for the Future

Week 5
Visioning for the Future

Preparing for the Session

Watch the DVD segment that you will view with participants this week, Visioning for the Future (3:50).

In this segment, author Mike Slaughter talks about the difference between seeing with your own human eyes and understanding and letting God reveal possibilities to you through the eyes of faith.

Mike says, "It's critical everyday that I take time and vision the future. When you come to the place where you see the best things in the past, you're dead."

"Visioning is seeing through the eyes of faith not the eyes of your head."

Using his congregation as an example, Mike shares how the original, small group at Ginghamsburg twenty years ago could see the potential they had for affecting the world around them. Mike tells about the new vision his congregation has had for building homes for older foster parents and at-risk children, brought together through the possibilities seen by the congregation.

"I have more energy and vision and desire to continue ministry . . . than I did at 26 because of these disciplines I practice in my life everyday."

Participant DVD Journal: You may also want to familiarize yourself with the Participant DVD Journal that participants are encouraged to use in their personal time. You may wish to share the following tip with participants choosing to use this resource:

TIP FIVE: Get ready to spend some time in your Bible by looking at biblical examples of *microscopic* and *telescopic* vision. There is also a goal-setting worksheet and overview of how to set goals as you look at a God-directed future. Plus, view another message from Mike Slaughter and spend time in prayer.

Icebreaker *(5 minutes)*

Read the following aloud:

Today we will be talking about the importance of vision. Vision empowers us to sing songs of faith in the face of discouragement and resistance and keep moving forward toward God's promised future. When we grasp God's vision for our lives, we celebrate what is right with life. We focus on the positive, redemptive activity of God that is going on continually all around us. When we celebrate what's right, we build vision for God's possibilities and find energy to fix what's wrong. Let's begin our session today by focusing on what's right!

Invite each participant to share and celebrate "what's right" in his or her life. Encourage participants who are experiencing difficult or challenging times to look for some evidence of God's redemptive work around them.

Video *(6-10 minutes)*

(Running Time 3:50)

Group Discussion *(20-25 minutes)*

Note: *More questions are provided than you will have time to cover in the group session. Select from those provided to suit the needs and interests of your particular group.*

1. Discuss the purpose and power of vision. Why is it important for each of us to envision God's purpose and direction for our lives?
2. What are the three sequences in the vision process? Spend some time discussing the second sequence: *conceive.* How do we

conceive God's vision or purpose? What disciplines help us to do this?

3. What is the difference between a microscopic view and a telescopic view? Give some biblical and contemporary examples of each perspective.

4. Read Psalm 122:1-2. According to verse 1, what was the Israelite worshiper's intention? What does verse 2 tell us was the picture that the worshipers held in their heads? Why do you think it helped them to hold onto this vision of their destination?

5. Share your responses to the question, *What happens when we focus on and work toward God's promised destination?* (Workbook, p. 79). Has working toward God's promised destination ever led you to take "bold life actions"? Share as you are willing.

6. Why do you think so many people quit in the face of resistance and opposition rather than persevering until they realize the promise of God? How can we build daily on the promising picture of God's preferred future—rather than allowing what we see, hear, and feel to determine our future? Share some practical examples with one another.

7. In our fiercely independent culture, we tend to believe that we can make it on our own—that we can accomplish our dreams if only we put our minds to it. Why is this a dangerous—and false—assumption?

8. Read Mark 2:1-11. In what ways were the paralyzed man's friends faithful, persistent, innovative, and resourceful? Whose faith led Jesus to heal the paralyzed man?

9. Respond to the following statement: *We have more faith together than we do by ourselves; sometimes when it's too hard for us to trust God, other people can trust for us.* When has the faith or vision of others helped to sustain you on the journey of ascent?

10. Read James 3:5. What does this verse tell us about the power of the tongue? When we're tempted to point out what's wrong in a

situation, why is it important that we choose to "speak faith" instead?

11. What does it mean to "articulate an attitude of determined faith"? Share a time when you did this, and tell what happened.

12. Read Proverbs 29:18. What happens when people have no vision? Why do you think a lack of vision often leads to depression and hopelessness?

13. To what kind of people does God entrust vision? What determines the size of vision God gives an individual?

14. How does a strategic action plan help us to get closer to God's promised future? What are four categories we should consider when creating a strategic action plan?

Application Exercise (10-15 minutes)

Break into accountability groups and discuss the following: *What does the daily discipline of envisioning God's future involve? How can we intentionally envision God's purpose and direction for our lives?* Then come back together as a full group and have one person from each accountability group share the group's thoughts. As a group, commit to practice the discipline of visioning each day in the coming week.

Accountability Assignment (1-2 minutes)

Remind participants that vision is nurtured in community, and suggest that they encourage one another this week as they seek to envision God's future and complete (if they have not already done so) or review their strategic action plans. Encourage each participant to share his or her strategic action plan with at least one other member in the accountability group prior to the next group session.

Closing Prayer (1-2 minutes)

If our lives are to be an honorable, excellent offering to you, O God, we can never afford to become content or comfortable staying

where we are. We must continually move forward on a life-long journey of ascent. Compel us forward with the power of vision so that we
may become our best *in* the world and *for* the world. Keep us mindful
that life is too short to live for anything less than a fulfilling, fruitful,
and faithful purpose. May we take time every day to dream your dream
for our lives, and may we have the faith and courage to execute the
visions you give us. Amen.

Key Components of Session: Start Time

_____   _____

_____   _____

_____   _____

_____   _____

_____   _____

_____   _____

_____   _____

Three points I want to make:

1. _____

_____

_____

2. _____

_____

_____

3. _____

_____

_____

Prayer Requests:

_____

_____

_____

_____

_____

Week 6
Eating and Exercise for Life

Week 6
Eating and Exercise for Life

Preparing for the Session

Watch the DVD segment that you will view with participants this week, Eating and Exercise for Life (6:08).

In this video segment, author Mike Slaughter asks, "From a biblical perspective . . . we believe that our bodies are the temple of the Holy Spirit. When are we going to start treating them as if they are?"

Mike describes how he took better care of a car that he borrowed for a trip more than he cared for his own. What does that suggest about this body that belongs to God? Mike tells the group about his own physical crisis point in his mid-forties when cardiac distress caused his personal health conversion. For one year, he and his wife, Carolyn, worked with a personal trainer on the three "triangle legs" of health: eating, cardio exercise, and resistance training.

Eating: rather than dieting, Mike describes help he received in making good choices

Cardio exercise: heart healthy exercise like walking or running three to five times a week

Weight training or resistance exercise: building muscle through weight or resistance training three times a week to build bone density and muscle strength

"At 54, you can have more energy than you had at 34. It's how I know that at 80, I am going to be ripe for God to really use," he says.

Mike tells us that you can't take others beyond where you can take yourself.

Participant DVD Journal: You may also want to familiarize yourself with the Participant DVD Journal that participants are encouraged to use in their personal time. You may wish to share the following tip with participants choosing to use this resource:

TIP SIX: Check out these online resources to help you develop healthy habits. Do you know your Real Age? Take the online test and find out. There is also an inspirational poster you can print out—"I can do all things through Christ which strengtheneth me" (Philippians 4:13, KJV). And you can! You will find that out as you complete another Status Check of D-R-I-V-E. You will be amazed how far you have come.

Icebreaker (5 minutes)

Share with one another some of the things you love about life—things that add sparkle to your world. (Participants may refer to their responses on page 89 in the Workbook.)

Video (6-10 minutes)

(Running Time 6:08)

Group Discussion (20-25 minutes)

Note: More questions are provided than you will have time to cover in the group session. Select from those provided to suit the needs and interests of your particular group.

1. Read Genesis 2:7. What does this verse tell us about the uniqueness of human life? What does it tell us about our value to God?
2. Read 1 Corinthians 6:19-20. What does the apostle Paul mean when he says that our bodies are temples of the Holy Spirit? How should this awareness affect the decisions we make regarding the care of our bodies?
3. The author writes, "Eating healthy foods and making a disciplined commitment to exercise is not optional for the committed

follower of Jesus. It is one of the essential daily life *disciplines* of discipleship." How do Romans 12:1 and 2 Corinthians 7:1 support the idea that healthy eating and exercise habits should be an essential discipline of every disciple's life?

4. What does it mean to say that salvation is a lifestyle of (w)holiness? How is wholeness (in body, mind, and spirit) related to holiness?

5. How is the completion of God's mission in the world dependent upon our physical bodies? What are some practical ways that we can be the hands, feet, and mouth of Jesus in our world—in our homes, workplaces, communities, and beyond?

6. Read Psalm 128:5-6. What does the psalmist value in these verses? In what ways do our life choices affect our health and longevity? Share some examples from your own life or the lives of people you know.

7. Which of the six factors affecting longevity do you find most challenging, and why? (See Workbook, p. 94.)

8. Read Luke 4:1-13. In what ways was Jesus tempted to submit his mind and spirit to his appetite? What enabled him to overcome this temptation? How is our ability to have discipline over our physical bodies a "doorway" to all other disciplines in our lives?

9. Read 2 Samuel 11:1-5. How did David surrender to his passions, and what happened as a result? What enables us to exercise discipline over our physical bodies?

10. Discuss some of the excuses and rationalizations we use to avoid making a commitment to exercise and healthy eating. Share one of the underlying deceptions and corresponding truths you identified in Momentum Builder #4 (Workbook, pp. 103–04).

11. As you are willing, share your response to the question, *What are some ways you need to practice self-leadership in the area of your health?* (Workbook, p. 97).

12. What are the three triangle legs of a healthy lifestyle? Briefly discuss each one.

Application Exercise *(10-15 minutes)*

Break into accountability groups and share the goals you have set for yourself in the three triangle legs of a healthy lifestyle: good nutrition, aerobic exercise, and resistance training (Workbook, pp. 101–02). Discuss: *What kind of encouragement, assistance, and/or accountability will you need in order to reach your goals? Where/from whom will you seek to find this accountability/support?*

Accountability Assignment *(1-2 minutes)*

Encourage accountability groups to provide the initial encouragement and support for one another as they begin to pursue the goals they have set in the area of physical health. Although this is the final group session, suggest that group members "check in" with one another once a week for at least the next four weeks, sharing encouragement and progress reports. Some participants may even want to get together (on either a regular or occasional basis) to exercise or play a sport, participate in a nutrition/weight management program together, or exchange healthy recipes and other ideas.

Closing Prayer *(1-2 minutes)*

Holy God, we are awe-struck by the realization that our bodies are your dwelling place. They are not our own, for we have been purchased by your redemptive work through Jesus' life, death, and resurrection. Help us to honor you with our bodies—with how we care for them and how we make use of them. Teach us to be disciplined in our commitment to exercise and good nutrition so that we may be healthy and whole vessels ever ready to continue your work in the world. Empower us to exercise discipline over our bodies so that our minds and spirits will no longer be held hostage to our passions and appetites. From this day forward, may our bodies and our lives be honorable, excellent offerings to you, O God. Amen.

Key Components of Session: Start Time

_____ _____

_____ _____

_____ _____

_____ _____

_____ _____

_____ _____

_____ _____

Three points I want to make:

1. _____

_____

_____

2. _____

_____

_____

3. _____

_____

_____

Prayer Requests:

_____

_____

_____

_____

_____